ANIMAL LIVES

The Frog

KINGFISHER
Larousse Kingfisher Chambers Inc.
95 Madison Avenue
New York, New York 10016

First published in 2000
2 4 6 8 10 9 7 5 3 1

1TR(1SBF)/1199/SC/RPR(RPR)/150NYM

LIBRARY OF CONGRESS CATALOGING-IN-PUBLICATION DATA
Kitchen, Bert.
The Frog/illustrated by Bert Kitchen; written by Sally Tagholm.—1st ed.
p. cm.—(Animal Lives)
Summary: Describes the life cycle of frogs, discussing how they are born, develop,
feed, play, and breed.
ISBN 0-7534-5215-4
1. Frogs—Juvenile literature.[1. Frogs.] I. Tagholm, Sally. II. Title. III. Animal lives
(New York, N. Y.)
QL668.E2 K58 2000
597.8'9—dc21   99-047978

Series editor: Miranda Smith
Series designer: Sarah Goodwin

Printed in Hong Kong

ANIMAL LIVES
The Frog

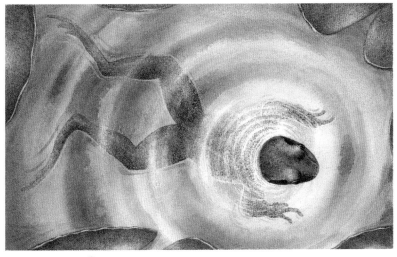

Illustrated by
Bert Kitchen

Written by
Sally Tagholm

KINGFISHER
NEW YORK

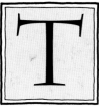The bright spring sun gently warms the undergrowth, drying the tiny drops of rain on the ferns and grass. It is time to wake up after the long, quiet winter. The smooth, speckled frog slips quietly out of the darkness and into the soft, warm air. He sits, blinking in the sunlight. He has been hibernating under a small rock at the bottom of a ditch — a safe, secret hiding place.

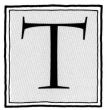he frog is hungry after his long sleep, but he waits patiently, perfectly camouflaged against the green shoots and old brown leaves. It is not long before he spots his first meal—a pink, juicy worm inching slowly through the soil. He bides his time, toes twitching. Then he pounces, seizing the wriggling prey in his wide mouth. He scrapes off the dirt with delicate fingers before gulping it down whole.

There is plenty of food to sustain him as he begins his journey—slugs, snails, and perhaps a spider or two. He leaps silently through the long grass, heading for the cool, fresh water of the pond that is his summer home. His strong back legs arch and stretch as they propel him high into the air, then fold beneath him as he lands, neatly hinged. A small, black fly dozing in the sun stops him in his tracks, and his long, sticky tongue darts out in a flash, scooping the insect greedily into his mouth.

It is not far to the pond, where the wild iris blooms and the lily pads float serenely on the water's dark surface. But the frog must be very careful. There are all kinds of hungry creatures lurking. Suddenly, he is surprised by the large hedgehog who nests in the leaves under the hollow oak tree. She chases him at an alarming speed, shuffling along on her short, stout legs, spines quivering. He narrowly escapes, launching himself through the air with his most athletic leaps until, at last, he plunges into the safety of the water.

He surfaces again briefly, curving up through the duckweed to snatch a gulp of air before diving back into the murky water. His strong hind legs slice smoothly behind him, their large webbed feet splayed out like slippery paddles. But soon he turns and heads back toward the sunshine. Clambering onto a lily pad, he joins the choir of male frogs each croaking to find a mate. It is a tuneless din that saws through the air like a rusty orchestra.

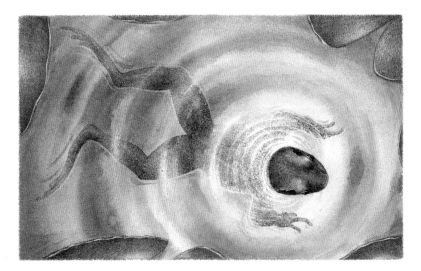

he pouch in his throat puffs up like a tiny balloon, turning each breath into an impressively loud croak. He doesn't even have to open his mouth or move his lips, so he can perform just as efficiently under water. Before long, a female responds, grunting quietly in reply. She hops gingerly down the steep bank, rustling through the meadowsweet and reeds. Her smooth, damp chest is red now, and her body is fat and bulging with eggs. Each year, like clockwork, she comes back to the pond for the breeding season. She moves slowly after her journey and slides carefully into the cool water to join her new mate. All around them, the croaky chorus continues, filling the spring air.

he pair swims side by side, graceful in the water. Soon, he climbs onto her, piggyback, clasping her firmly under the arms so his fingers meet across her chest. He has a special spiny patch on each thumb to help him get a good grip. They swim in this shadowy embrace for one whole day and one whole night before she releases her stream of eggs. The male fertilizes them before they sink to the bottom of the pond and the frogs part.

he tiny, black eggs have no shells, but are protected by a layer of jelly. This swells in the water, gluing the eggs together in a mass that floats up to the surface. The sun gently warms the frogspawn as the tadpoles grow, neatly curled inside their capsules—tempting food for ducks and fish. After two weeks, the tadpoles that survive will hatch and wriggle free into the water.

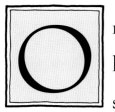Once they have left their floating nursery, the tiny, newly hatched tadpoles cling tightly to the nearest weeds, swaying this way and that, like extra leaves. After a few days, their mouths and eyes open and they dart off through the water, long tails wriggling, breathing through special, feathery gills just behind their heads. They swarm together in a school, eating a soup of slimy, green algae. But a fleet of predators lurks, including the newts who have also returned to the pond to breed.

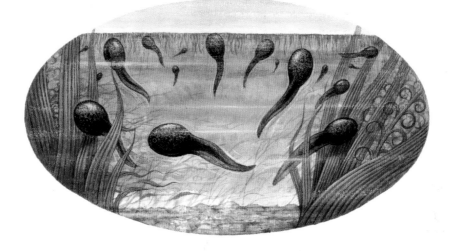

he tadpoles grow rapidly from day to day, and before long, they start to lose their familiar, slippery shape. They sprout miniature back legs, fully jointed and froglike, with tiny webbed feet. Lungs develop inside their small bodies, and smooth, new skin covers the gills they no longer need. They swim to the surface—odd, in-between creatures, no longer tadpoles but not yet frogs—and help themselves to floating insects and grubs. Within a month, their short front legs will appear, elbows first, turning them into tiny froglets with wriggling tails.

It is midsummer now, and the thick reeds stretch their long, green fingers high in the blue sky. The tadpoles have turned into perfectly formed, miniature frogs, no bigger than a baby's fingernail. It will be another three years before they are fully grown. Their tails have slowly shrunk and vanished, and they have shed their old, tight tadpole skins. They have already started to hop out of the water and sit like tiny, shiny statues on the smooth, gray rocks. Soon, they will swarm onto the banks of the pond, ready to investigate the world beyond.

But the froglets are defenseless, and few will survive to adulthood. They are at the mercy of many creatures, both in the water and on land. They must be especially careful of the tall, gray herons who stalk through the shadows, stabbing the water with their long, yellow bills. They are feeding their young and need plenty of beetles, water voles—and tender, young froglets!

The breeding season is over and the adult frogs are quiet now, peering out from their hiding places around the pond. Others, submerged in duckweed, watch with periscope eyes as froglets hop high in the air like tiny acrobats. Below the surface, tadpoles of all shapes and sizes—some freshly hatched, others almost fully formed— grow to adulthood.

THE COMMON FROG

Scientific name: *Rana temporaria*

Size: Adult males are approximately 3 inches long. Adult females are approximately 3.5 inches long.

Distribution: This species is found in Europe and Asia, but frogs live on all continents except Antarctica. Close relatives in North America include the bullfrog, the green frog, the leopard frog, the tree frog, and the spadefoot toad.

Habitat: Damp grass, undergrowth, ditches, ponds.

Food: Insects, slugs, snails, earthworms, caterpillars, spiders.

Predators: Fish, rats, otters, hedgehogs, badgers, newts, snakes, herons, owls.

Special characteristics: Smooth, moist skin that helps absorb oxygen, strong hind legs with webbed feet, protruding eyes with transparent lids and excellent vision in all directions, and a long, sticky tongue.

Call: Each species of frog has a unique call so that only members of the same species will react to it. It is produced by the male frog filling his lungs with air, then closing his mouth and nostrils. The air moves back and forth from the lungs to the inflated vocal pouch over the vocal chords, creating a croaking sound.

ABOUT THE FROG

The common frog is found in Europe and the cooler parts of Asia, but it has close relatives scattered all over the world. These include flying frogs that can glide through the rain forest, and spadefoot frogs that burrow underground. The largest frog in the world is the Goliath frog of West Africa, which can be up to 12 inches in length. One of the smallest frogs lives in Brazil and is only half an inch long.

AFRICAN REED FROG
These African frogs have an especially loud croak that can be heard several miles away. They need to make a loud noise to attract a mate because they live in tall reeds and are difficult to see.

TREE FROG

Tree frogs are usually smaller than frogs that live on the ground so that they can climb more easily. They have small suckers on their long toes to help them get a good grip. Tree frogs live in much of North America and other warm areas.

SOUTH AMERICAN ARROW POISON FROG
Unlike most other frogs, these do not escape from danger by hiding or leaping away. Instead, they use their brilliantly colored markings to show that they are dangerous to eat. Their skin is so poisonous that some South American Indians use the poison for their blow guns.

FROG WORDS

algae microscopic water plants that look like green slime

amphibian a creature that lives both on land and in water

breeding season the time of year when mating occurs

froglet a tiny, fully formed frog

frogspawn a mass of frogs' eggs enclosed in jelly

gills the external organs through which tadpoles breathe by taking oxygen from the water they live in

hibernate to sleep through the winter

predator a creature that hunts and kills for food

prey a creature that is hunted for food

tadpole a tiny, long-tailed frog hatchling that lives under water

webbed feet feet with toes joined together by skin

FOR FURTHER INFORMATION

National Reptile and Amphibian Advisory Council
nraac@kingsnake.com
www.thevivarium.com

Rainforest Action Network
221 Pine Street, Suite 500
San Francisco, CA 94104
www.ran.org

Center for North American Amphibians and Reptiles
1502 Medinah Circle
Lawrence, KS 66047
(785) 749 3467

Virtual Frog Dissection Kit
george.lbl.gov/vfrog

INDEX

ACKNOWLEDGMENTS

The author and publishers thank Muriel Kitchen and John Tagholm for the photographs on the jacket.